The Magician's Nephew

A Reading Comprehension Guide

by
Kathy Mahaffy
and David Kohl

About the Author

Kathy Mahaffy taught third grade and now teaches high school at Logos School in Moscow, Idaho. She graduated from the University of Idaho with a degree in Elementary Education. She has four children and attends the Evangelical Free Church of Pullman.

Logos School Literature Series

Resources for Reading Comprehension, Writing, and Spelling

C109 Reading Comprehension: The Magician's Nephew ISBN 1-930443-45-5

Cover design by Paige Atwood Design, Moscow, Idaho
Original cover art by Elisabeth Ryan, a 6th grade student at Logos School

Logos School Materials 110 Baker Street Moscow, Idaho 83843

Call Toll Free 866-562-2174 for a free catalog or visit www.logosschool.com

Suggestions for use

This booklet contains a comprehension sheet for each chapter, answer keys, a vocabulary list, a creative writing assignment, crossword and juggle puzzles, and a final test.

Before reading a chapter, it is encouraged that the student look up the definitions for the vocabulary words corresponding to that chapter. If it is difficult to find the definition in the dictionary, the student may find the meaning in the context of his reading.

In order for the students to know what is expected of them, some instruction will be needed before beginning the comprehension questions. The following six-point grading scale is used:

1. One point is awarded when the student begins his answer with a capital letter.

2. One point is awarded when the student ends his answer with an end mark.

3. One point is awarded when the student restates the question in the answer. For example, if the question reads, "Who is the author of the book?", the answer should be, "The author of the book is C. S. Lewis."

4. A correct answer is worth anywhere from one to three points. This allows the teacher to give partial credit for an answer that is not completely correct.

In order to make this booklet more useful to a wider group of abilities, a section entitled **"A Bit More..."** has been added to the basic comprehension questions. These questions should be used by students at a higher grammar level or as discussion questions for lower grammar level students.

The answer keys at the end of this booklet contain the main element that needs to be present in order to answer the question correctly.

Understanding vocabulary is vital to comprehending what is being read. The following four step exercise gives meaning to the unfamiliar vocabulary:

Step 1: Find the word in the chapter and write it out in context. This may be done by writing the complete sentence where the word is found or, if the sentence is too lengthy, by writing a few of the words on either side of the vocabulary word.

Step 2: Guess the meaning from the context and write it down.

Step 3: Look the word up in the dictionary and write the definition.

Step 4: Use the word in a sentence.

In order to reinforce learning of the vocabulary words, the student should do one of the following after reading the chapter:

1. Write original sentences using each of the vocabulary words correctly, or...

2. Write a brief explanation of how the word is used in the chapter.

The creative writing assignment is included to give the student an opportunity to hone their writing skills. This assignment may be tailored to focus on skills being taught in the student's English curriculum. (Descriptive or narrative writing, for example.)

The puzzles included are for fun and review!

The student should take the test after finishing the book. The test may be taken using the book and should be graded as follows:

1. Each item in the **Matching** section is worth one point.

2. Each blank in the **Fill in the Blank** section is worth one point.

3. Each answer in the **Short Answer** section should be graded in the same way as the comprehension questions for each individual chapter.

The Magician's Nephew

C. S. Lewis

Introduction

Fill out the following information about this book:

TITLE: _____

AUTHOR: _____

ILLUSTRATOR: _____

PUBLISHER: _____

This book is an example of: FICTION   NON-FICTION   POETRY   (circle one)

For the following chapters, list the title and the page number where you would find the chapter.

Chapter	Title	Page
3	_____	_____
8	_____	_____
11	_____	_____
15	_____	_____

The Magician's Nephew

C. S. Lewis

Name: _____
Date: _____

Chapter 1: The Wrong Door

1. Why was Digory living with his Uncle Andrew and Aunt Letty? _____

_____

_____

2. Where were Polly and Digory going when they walked through the tunnel? _____

_____

_____

3. Whom did the children find in the furnished room? _____

_____

_____

4. What did Polly touch, and what happened to her? _____

_____

_____

A Bit More...

5. What is peculiar about Uncle Andrew? _____

_____

_____

_____

The Magician's Nephew

C. S. Lewis

Chapter 2: Digory and His Uncle

1. What did Mrs. Lefay give to Uncle Andrew, and what was in it? _____

_____

_____

2. What happened if someone touched the dust? _____

_____

_____

3. What was the use of a green ring? _____

_____

_____

4. Why did Digory go to the Otherworld? _____

_____

_____

A Bit More...

5. Why wouldn't Uncle Andrew test the rings himself? _____

_____

_____

_____

continued...

6. Why does Uncle Andrew think it's permissible for himself to lie but not Digory? Explain why you agree or disagree.

_____

_____

_____

_____

_____

The Magician's Nephew

C. S. Lewis

Name: _____
Date: _____

Chapter 3: The Wood Between the Worlds

1. What did Digory see when he arrived in the Otherworld? _____

_____

_____

2. Of what other place did the wood remind Digory? _____

_____

_____

3. What did Digory want to do before going back home? _____

_____

_____

4. How did the children mark the pool that would take them home? _____

_____

_____

A Bit More...

5. Uncle Andrew was wrong about how the rings actually did work. Explain how he was wrong and

what was correct. _____

_____

_____

continued...

The Magician's Nephew
C.S. Lewis

Chapter 3: **The Wood Between the Worlds**

Common Nouns: Remember that a noun is a person, place, or thing, and that many times it is indicated by one of the article adjectives: a, an, the. Write a sentence using each of the following vocabulary words. <u>Underline</u> the **nouns** that you've used in the sentence.

1. muddled: _____

_____

2. glimpse: _____

_____

3. horrid: _____

_____

4. apparently: _____

_____

5. pluck: _____

_____

6. chimney-pot: _____

_____

7. vague: _____

_____

8. landmark: _____

_____

9. turf: _____

_____

10. solemn: _____

_____

The Magician's Nephew

C. S. Lewis

Name: _____
Date: _____

Chapter 4: **The Bell and the Hammer**

1. What was strange about the new world? _____

_____

_____

2. What did the children find in the room? _____

_____

_____

3. As they walked down the row ,what did the children notice about the people ? _____

_____

_____

4. What did Digory find on the square pillar? _____

_____

_____

5. What happened when Digory hit the bell? _____

_____

_____

A Bit More...

6. Explain in your own words the meaning of the poem inscribed on the pillar. _____

_____

_____

_____

_____

The Magician's Nephew

C. S. Lewis

Chapter 5: The Deplorable Word

1. Who was the beautiful woman who came back to life? _____

_____

_____

_____

2. How did Jadis win the war against her sister? _____

_____

_____

_____

3. What did Jadis want to do with Digory and Polly? Why? _____

_____

_____

_____

4. Who did Jadis think that Uncle Andrew was? _____

_____

_____

_____

The Magician's Nephew
C.S. Lewis

Chapter 5: The Deplorable Word

Verbs: Remember that a verb is a word that asserts action. Write the definitions for the verbs listed below. You may find the definition from the context of the chapter or look up the word in the dictionary.

1. facing _____

2. trembling _____

3. forced _____

4. mentioning _____

5. collapsing _____

6. fastened _____

7. seizing _____

8. vanished _____

9. blotted _____

10. seek _____

11. freed _____

12. stammered _____

13. fetch _____

14. prepare _____

15. plunged _____

The Magician's Nephew

C. S. Lewis

Name: _____
Date: _____

Chapter 6: The Beginning of Uncle Andrew's Troubles

1. How did the Queen get to the Wood and then to London? _____

_____

_____

2. According to Queen Jadis, what kind of Magician was Uncle Andrew? _____

_____

_____

3. Why did the Queen take notice of Uncle Andrew and not Digory? _____

_____

_____

4. Why did Uncle Andrew change his clothes? _____

_____

_____

A Bit More...

5. How is Uncle Andrew like Jadis? How are they different? _____

_____

_____

_____

The Magician's Nephew

C. S. Lewis

Name: _____
Date: _____

Chapter 7: What Happened at the Front Door

1. Since some of Jadis' powers did not work in this world, what did she do to Aunt Letty? _____

_____

_____

2. When a lady brought grapes for Digory's mother, what did he begin thinking about? _____

_____

_____

3. How did the Queen arrive back at the house? _____

_____

_____

4. Why was the policeman following Jadis? _____

_____

_____

A Bit More...

5. What kind of a person is Aunt Letty? What does she think of Jadis? _____

_____

_____

_____

continued...

The Magician's Nephew
C.S. Lewis

Chapter 7: **What Happened at the Front Door**

Adjectives: An adjective is a word that describes a noun. It answers the questions, "What kind?", "Which one?", and "How many?". For the following nouns, write an adjective that describes it by answering the questions asked.

What kind?

Example: magnificent jump

1. _____ thoughts

2. _____ language

3. _____ room

4. _____ dinner

5. _____ things

6. _____ eyes

Which one?

Example: this moment

7. _____ land

8. _____ buses

How many?

Example: single glance

9. _____ moment(s)

10. _____ people

11. _____ hansom(s)

12. _____ house(s)

The Magician's Nephew

C. S. Lewis

Chapter 8: The Fight at the Lamp-Post

1. Who all traveled to the Wood? _____

_____

_____

2. Describe the empty world as the group first arrived. _____

_____

_____

3. How did the Cabby suggest they pass the time? _____

_____

_____

4. What two wonders happened at the same time? _____

_____

_____

5. As the sun came up, whom did the group see as the Singer? _____

_____

_____

A Bit More...

6. Is the Cabby a good man? Explain. _____

_____

_____

_____

The Magician's Nephew

C. S. Lewis

Name: _____

Date: _____

Chapter 9: The Founding of Narnia

1. What did Polly notice about the Lion's song? _____

_____

_____

2. What did the Witch do with the iron bar, and how did the Lion react? _____

_____

_____

3. What became of the iron bar? _____

_____

_____

4. Why did Digory go after the Lion? _____

_____

_____

5. What was created from the Lion's wilder song? _____

_____

_____

A Bit More...

6. What was Uncle Andrew thinking when Aslan was singing? _____

_____

_____

_____

The Magician's Nephew
C.S. Lewis

Chapter 9: **The Founding of Narnia**

Adverbs: An adverb describes a verb. It answers the questions "How?", "When?", and "Where?". For the following verbs, write an adverb that describes it by answering the questions asked.

How?

Example: treated <u>abominably</u>

1. spread   _____

2. said   _____

3. swayed   _____

4. stepped   _____

5. turned   _____

6. beat   _____

7. faded   _____

When?

Example: ate <u>later</u>

8. left   _____

9. see   _____

10. turn   _____

Where?

Example: looked <u>up</u>

11. spread   _____

12. came   _____

13. backing   _____

14. walked   _____

15. darted   _____

The Magician's Nephew

C. S. Lewis

Chapter 10: The First Joke and Other Matters

1. What happened when Aslan breathed on the animals in the circle? _____

_____

_____

2. Why did Aslan call his council together? _____

_____

_____

3. What did the Cabby ask Strawberry to do? _____

_____

_____

4. What did Uncle Andrew hear when the animals spoke? _____

_____

_____

A Bit More...

5. Why was Uncle Andrew unable to hear what Digory, Polly, and the Cabby heard? _____

_____

_____

_____

The Magician's Nephew

C. S. Lewis

Chapter 11: Digory and his Uncle are Both in Trouble

1. What did the animals do to Uncle Andrew, and why did they do it? _____

_____

_____

2. What did Aslan call Digory? _____

_____

3. Aslan asked Digory how the Witch had come to Narnia. What was Digory's answer? _____

_____

_____

4. Why did Aslan bring the Cabby's wife to Narnia? _____

_____

_____

A Bit More...

5. List the questions Aslan asks the Cabby to see if he is fit to be King of Narnia. (Use your own words.)

_____

_____

_____

_____

6. What qualifications do you think someone needs to have in order to be a good king? _____

_____

_____

_____

_____

continued...

Chapter 11: Digory and His Uncle Are Both in Trouble

Synonyms: Match each word with the correct partner of similar meaning.

1.	frock	_____	answered
2.	vague	_____	happy
3.	toppled	_____	serious
4.	replied	_____	dim
5.	dispute	_____	leave
6.	withered	_____	shrunk
7.	revived	_____	hit
8.	solemn	_____	dress
9.	struck	_____	retrieved
10.	merry	_____	crowning
11.	astonished	_____	argument
12.	fetched	_____	fell
13.	imitation	_____	surprised
14.	retreat	_____	fake
15.	coronation	_____	awakened

The Magician's Nephew

C. S. Lewis

Name: _____
Date: _____

Chapter 12: Strawberry's Adventure

1. What task did Aslan give Digory to "undo the wrong" Digory had done to Narnia? _____

_____

_____

_____

2. How would Digory get to the garden in the valley? _____

_____

_____

3. What did Fledge and the children eat for supper? _____

_____

_____

4. Where did Digory and Polly sleep? _____

_____

_____

A Bit More...

5. Digory and Polly heard something strange. What do you think it was? _____

_____

_____

The Magician's Nephew

C. S. Lewis

Chapter 13: An Unexpected Meeting

1. What had grown up overnight? _____

_____

_____

2. What was Digory tempted to do in the garden? What might have stopped him? _____

_____

_____

3. Whom did Digory see in the garden, and what was she doing? _____

_____

_____

4. What two things did the Witch ask Digory to do? _____

_____

_____

A Bit More...

5. Explain the poem on the gate in your own words. _____

_____

_____

_____

6. Think of an example where someone could find "their heart's desire and find despair." (How would

someone get what they wanted and still despair?) _____

_____

_____

_____

_____

7. What Bible story is this chapter like? _____

_____

_____

continued...

Antonyms: Match each word with the correct partner of opposite meaning.

1. honesty   _____ genius

2. rushing   _____ defeated

3. stooping   _____ gracefully

4. steep   _____ lagging

5. awkwardly   _____ loudest

6. private   _____ deception

7. faintest   _____ dislike

8. horrid   _____ public

9. triumphant   _____ kind

10. vanish   _____ level

11. simpleton   _____ pleasant

12. cruel   _____ allow

13. prevent   _____ limited

14. fond   _____ straightening

15. endless   _____ appear

The Magician's Nephew

C. S. Lewis

Chapter 14: The Planting of the Tree

1. Where was Uncle Andrew? _____

_____

_____

2. What gift did Aslan give to Uncle Andrew, and how did he give it? _____

_____

_____

3. What was the purpose of the tree Digory planted, and how did it work? _____

_____

_____

4. What did Aslan give to Digory? _____

_____

_____

A Bit More...

5. Aslan says, concerning the witch, "All get what they want: they do not always like it." Explain how

this is true in her case. _____

_____

_____

The Magician's Nephew

C. S. Lewis

Chapter 15: The End of the Story and the Beginning of All the Others

1. What was Aslan's warning to the children? _____

_____

_____

2. What command did Aslan give to the children? _____

_____

_____

3. What did Digory do with the apple core? _____

_____

_____

4. Explain how the lamp-post and the tree in Digory's back garden connect this story with the other books in the series.

Lamp-Post: _____

_____

_____

Tree: _____

_____

_____

A Bit More...

5. What became of the following people:

Digory's mother: _____

_____

_____

Digory's father: _____

_____

_____

Uncle Andrew: _____

_____

_____

Polly: _____

_____

_____

Digory: _____

_____

_____

Chapter 15: The End of This Story

Punctuation & Capitalization: Correct the punctuation and capitalization errors. Remember to capitalize proper nouns and the first word of a sentence. Add endmarks, commas, and quotation marks.

1. come said aslan it is time that you went back

_____

2. let the race of adam and eve take warning

_____

3. both the children were looking up into the lion s face as he spoke these words

_____

4. i want to go to mother

_____

5. everyone of them even the sunlight looked faded and dingy

_____

6. they got a trowel and buried all the magic rings in a circle round it

_____

7. aunt letty did everything mother liked

_____

8. king frank and queen helen and their children lived happily in narnia

_____

9. and though he himself did not discover the magic properties of that wardrobe someone else did

_____

10. a devilish temper she had he would say

_____

The Magician's Nephew

Answer Key

Chapter 1:

1. Digory was living with his Uncle Andrew and Aunt Letty because his mother was dying and they were taking care of her.
2. Polly and Digory were trying to get to the empty house on the other side of Digory's house when they walked through the tunnel.
3. The children found Uncle Andrew in the furnished room.
4. Polly touched a yellow ring, and then she disappeared.
5. Uncle Andrew seemed peculiar because he had awful eyes, a mop of gray hair, and long white fingers. People thought that he was mad. He had a study in which no one was allowed to go. He also performed strange experiments.

Chapter 2:

1. Mrs. Lefay gave Uncle Andrew an old box filled with dust from another world.
2. If someone touched the dust, they would be drawn back to the place from which the dust came.
3. If someone used the green ring, it would bring them back to their world.
4. Digory went to the Otherworld to find Polly and bring her back.
5. Uncle Andrew didn't test the rings himself because he said that, since he was performing the experiments, he shouldn't participate in them, but actually he was a coward.
6. Uncle Andrew thought that it was permissible for himself to lie because he believed that great thinkers who had great wisdom didn't have to follow common rules. Answers will vary as to why they agree/disagree.

Chapter 3:

1. Digory saw many trees, small pools, and a green light when he arrived in the Otherworld.
2. The wood reminded Digory of the tunnel under the slates at home.
3. Digory wanted to jump into other pools and explore other worlds before going back home.
4. The children marked the pool that would take them home by cutting a long piece of turf by the side of the pool.
5. Uncle Andrew was wrong about how the rings worked because he thought that the yellow rings took people out of the real world and that the green rings brought them home. Actually the yellow rings took people into the Wood and the green rings took them to other worlds outside of the Wood.

Chapter 3 - Common Nouns:

Various answers

Chapter 4:
1. The new world seemed strange because there was a strange red light, empty crumbling buildings, and silence everywhere.
2. The children found hundreds of people sitting like statues in the room.
3. The children noticed, as they walked down the row, that the people at the beginning of the row looked kind and wise; but as they continued on, the faces began to look solemn and then cruel.
4. Digory found a golden bell and a hammer on the square pillar.
5. When Digory hit the bell, it made a noise which grew louder and louder and caused part of the roof to fall in.
6. The meaning of the poem inscribed on the pillar was this - Choose one of these two things: hit the bell and wait for the danger to come, or don't hit it and go crazy wondering what might have happened.

Chapter 5:
1. The beautiful woman who came back to life was Jadis, Queen of Charn.
2. Jadis won the war against her sister by using the Deplorable Word, which killed every living thing under the sun.
3. Jadis wanted Digory and Polly to take her to their world so she could rule it.
4. Jadis thought that Uncle Andrew was a great Magician, the king of their world.

Chapter 5 - Verbs

1. to look forward
2. to quiver or shake
3. to compel or produce by effort
4. to speak of
5. to fall or give way
6. to attach or fix
7. to grasp or lay hold of
8. to disappear
9. to obliterate
10. to make a search for
11. to set at liberty
12. to speak with repetitions of syllables
13. to go for and bring
14. to make ready
15. to enter or move forward with violence

Chapter 6:
1. The Queen got to the Wood by grabbing Polly's hair as she touched the yellow ring. She arrived in London by grabbing Digory's ear.
2. Queen Jadis said that Uncle Andrew was a Magician who works by rules and books, with no real Magic in his heart.
3. The Queen took notice of Uncle Andrew and not Digory because witches only take notice of people they can use.
4. Uncle Andrew changed his clothes because he imagined that the Witch may fall in love with him.
5. Answers will vary, but look for these things: Jadis is a real magician, but Uncle Andrew is a book magician; Jadis is very frightening, but Uncle Andrew is not as frightening when compared to her; Both are liars and want others to serve them.

Chapter 7:
1. Since Jadis' powers did not work in this world, she picked Letty up over her head and threw her across the room.
2. When a lady brought grapes for Digory's mother, he began to think about going to another world and finding fruit that would cure his mother.
3. The Queen returned to the house by standing on the roof of a hansom cab and driving the horse.
4. The policeman was following Jadis because a man had accused her of stealing a necklace.
5. Aunt Letty seems to be a proper woman who expects people to have good manners. She thinks Jadis is a woman of low character who might be drunk.

Chapter 7 - Adjectives

Various answers

Chapter 8:

1. Digory, Polly, the Queen, Uncle Andrew, the Cabby, and his horse all traveled to the Wood.
2. In the empty world there were complete darkness, no sound, and no wind.
3. The Cabby suggested that they pass the time by singing a hymn.
4. The voice was joined by other voices, and at the same time, thousands of stars appeared.
5. As the sun came up, the group saw a Lion singing.
6. Yes, the Cabby seems to be a good man because he is kind to Jadis and tries to help her. He is also kind to his horse. He is thankful that no one was hurt in the fall and suggests they sing a hymn of thanksgiving.

Chapter 9:

1. Polly noticed that, as she listened to the Lion's song, she heard the things he was creating.
2. The Witch threw the iron bar at the Lion and hit him. He acted as if nothing had happened.
3. The iron bar grew into a lamp-post.
4. Digory went after the Lion because he wanted to ask the Lion if he could help heal Digory's mother.
5. Animals were created from the Lion's wilder song.
6. When Aslan was singing, Andrew was thinking of ways he could take advantage of the new world. Ex. - Grow engines and ships to make money, build a sanatorium, etc.

Chapter 9 - Adverbs

Various answers

Chapter 10:

1. When Aslan breathed on the animals in the circle, they became Talking Beasts.
2. Aslan called his council together to talk because an evil had already entered the new world.
3. The Cabby asked Strawberry to give Digory a ride on his back to Aslan.
4. When the animals spoke, Uncle Andrew could not hear the words, only animal sounds.
5. Uncle Andrew had disliked the song because of the way it made him think and feel. He chose to pretend that the singing was roaring, and soon that was all he could hear and not what Digory, Polly, and the Cabby heard.

Chapter 11:

1. The animals planted Uncle Andrew in the ground and watered him because they thought that he was a tree.
2. Aslan called Digory a "Son of Adam."
3. When Aslan asked Digory how the Witch had come to Narnia, Digory answered that he had brought her by using the magic rings after he had awakened her with the golden bell.
4. Aslan brought the Cabby's wife to Narnia because he wanted the Cabby and his wife to live in Narnia as the first King and Queen.
5. Aslan asked the Cabby the following questions to see if he was fit to be the King of Narnia: A) Can he farm?, B) Can he treat the animals kindly?, C) Would he teach his children to treat the animals kindly?, D) Would he treat everyone fairly and not show favoritism?, and E) Would he be brave in leading a battle against his enemies?
6. Answers will vary.

Chapter 11 – Synonyms:

1. frock
2. vague
3. toppled
4. replied
5. dispute
6. withered
7. revived
8. solemn
9. struck
10. merry
11. astonished
12. fetched
13. imitation
14. retreat
15. coronation

4	answered
10	happy
8	serious
2	dim
14	leave
6	shrunk
9	hit
1	dress
12	retrieved
15	crowning
5	argument
3	fell
11	surprised
13	fake
7	awakened

Chapter 12:

1. Aslan gave Digory the task of plucking an apple from a tree, and bringing it to him to "undo the wrong" Digory had done to Narnia.
2. Digory would get to the garden in the valley by riding on Strawberry (Fledge), who was now a winged horse.
3. Fledge ate grass, and the children ate some toffee from Polly's pocket.
4. Digory and Polly slept under Fledge's wings.
5. Answers will vary.

Chapter 13:

1. A tree with toffee-like fruit grew up overnight.
2. Digory was tempted to eat some fruit. He saw a bird roosting in the tree, and it may have stopped him.
3. Digory saw the Witch in the garden eating some fruit.
4. The Witch asked Digory to eat the fruit and live forever. She also asked him to take the fruit to his mother to make her well.
5. The poem on the gate said to come in through the gates or stay out. Use the fruit for other people or don't take it. Those who steal the fruit or come in over the wall will get what they want but will end up unhappy.
6. Answers will vary. Look for reasons why the example works.
7. This chapter is like the Bible story of the temptation of Adam and Eve.

Chapter 13 - Antonyms:

1. honesty	_11_	genius
2. rushing	_9_	defeated
3. stooping	_5_	gracefully
4. steep	_2_	lagging
5. awkwardly	_7_	loudest
6. private	_1_	deception
7. faintest	_14_	dislike
8. horrid	_6_	public
9. triumphant	_12_	kind
10. vanish	_4_	level
11. simpleton	_8_	pleasant
12. cruel	_13_	allow
13. prevent	_15_	limited
14. fond	_3_	straightening
15. endless	_10_	appear

Chapter 14:
1. Uncle Andrew was in a cage made of a tangle of trees.
2. Aslan gave Uncle Andrew the gift of sleep by breathing on him.
3. The purpose of the tree Digory planted was to protect Narnia from the Witch. She would not come near because the smell of the tree was despair to her.
4. Aslan gave Digory an apple to take to his mother to make her well.
5. Jadis got what she wanted - great strength and a long life, but she will be miserable living a long time with an evil heart.

Chapter 15:
1. Aslan's warning to the children was to not let their world become as wicked as Charn.
2. The command Aslan gave to the children was to bury all of the magic rings when they got home.
3. Digory buried the apple core in the back garden.
4. The lamp-post became the place where another child entered Narnia. The wood from the tree was made into a wardrobe with magic properties.
5. Digory's mother became well again. Digory's father inherited money and a country house where Digory's family moved and lived. Uncle Andrew went to live with Digory's family. Polly remained friends with Digory and visited him at his house in the country. Digory became a professor and continued to live in the country-house. We will meet him again in another story.

Chapter 15 - Punctuation & Capitalization:
1. "Come," said Aslan, "It is time that you went back."
2. Let the race of Adam and Eve take warning.
3. Both the children were looking up into the lion's face as he spoke these words.
4. I want to go to Mother.
5. Everyone of them, even the sunlight, looked faded and dingy.
6. They got a trowel and buried all the magic rings in a circle round it.
7. Aunt Letty did everything Mother liked.
8. King Frank and Queen Helen and their children lived happily in Narnia.
9. And though he himself did not discover the magic properties of that wardrobe, someone else did.
10. "A devilish temper she had," he would say.

The Magician's Nephew

Vocabulary List

Chapter 1
grubby
indignantly
chiefly
cistern
smuggler
feeble
sitting-room
grate (noun)
pantomime
tousled
humor (verb)
cunning

Chapter 2
queer
asylum
ignorant
bureau
profound
sages
charwoman
harp (verb)
preposterous
adept
chivalry

Chapter 3
muddled
glimpse
horrid
apparently
pluck (noun)
chimney-pot
vague
landmark
turf
solemn

Chapter 4
eclipse
keen
threshold
avalanche
mere
dreary
ajar
enchantment
bide
dotty
obstinate
masonry

Chapter 5
pincers
peril
sulky
dismal
deplorable
accursed
aghast
contemptuous
incantations
potent
bosh
minions

Chapter 6
stooped
stifled
spitefully
shamming
pooh
procure
treachery
ghastly
sarcastically
pax
hansom
deucedly

Chapter 7
cowered
rubbish
hussy
rampaging
twopence
mutton
throttle (verb)
flogging
constable
ticklish
bowler

Chapter 8
brandished
brute
delirium
doom
flask
vengeance
impertinent
constellations
triumphant
uncivilized
cunningly

Chapter 9
lilting
nuisance
abominably
ostentatious
plucky
proportion
stupendous
sanatorium
chemist
stags
erect

Chapter 10
faun
satyr
naiad
cherish
perky
jackdaw
repress
hither
thicket
din

Chapter 11
frock
sovereigns (noun)
dispute (noun)
sagacious
revived
abide
chap (noun)
spade (noun)
coronation
desolate

Chapter 12
despair
fawny
grief
shied
curveted
heave
moorland
alighted
dismount
upheaval

Chapter 13
cataracts
glacier
gliding
forbear
hastily
roosting
saffron
pelt (verb)
simpleton
fatal
cantering

Chapter 14
conceited
switches (noun)
persuaded
coop
bombarded
christened
folly
torments (noun)
anvil
bellows
flourishes (verb)
loathe

Chapter 15
tyrants
bustling
wardrobe
counterpane
dingy
banisters
trowel
fortnight
frowsy
quivered
billiard-room

The Magician's Nephew

Creative Writing

Directions: When Digory and Polly are in the Wood, they realize that jumping into the pools will take them to new worlds. Write a story imagining that you have a yellow ring in one pocket and a green ring in the other. Jump into a pool and discover a new world. Describe what the world looks like, what people and creatures you might meet, and what adventures you might experience. Give your story a interesting title!

_____

Title

_____

_____

_____

_____

_____

_____

_____

_____

_____

_____

_____

_____

_____

_____

_____

_____

_____

The Magician's Nephew

Crossword Puzzle

Name: _____

Date: _____

Across

1. Became the King of Narnia
3. A very proper lady
6. Gave Digory and Polly a ride on his back
8. The children entered the Wood through this
11. Healing fruit
12. An enchanted world
13. Wanted a healing apple

Down

2. Awakened Jadis from her sleep
4. Made magic rings
5. Eaten for supper by the children
7. Created the new world with a song
8. Digory's friend
9. Was destroyed by the Deplorable Word
10. Queen of Charn
14. One green, one yellow

The Magician's Nephew

Crossword Answer Key

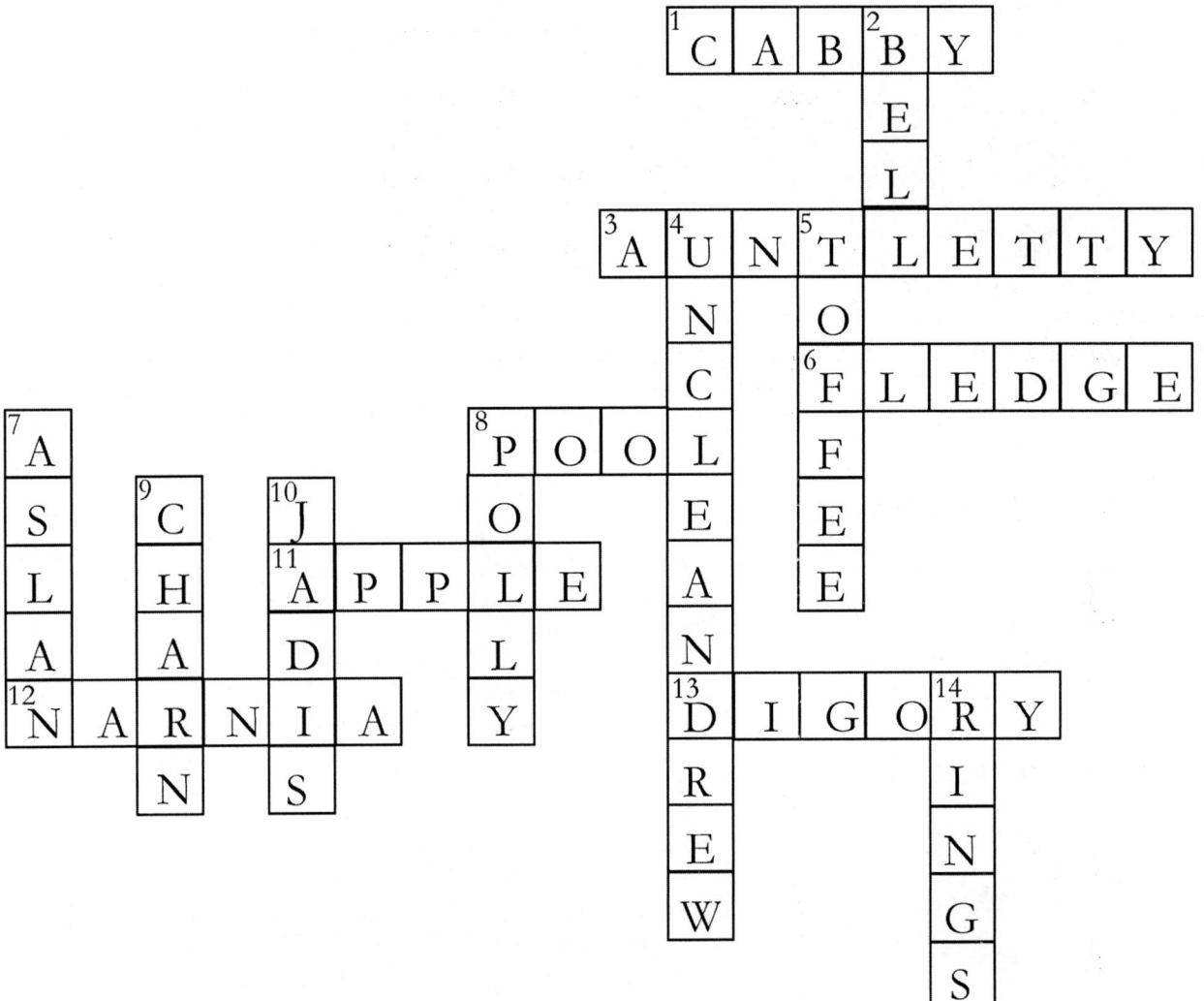

The Magician's Nephew

Name: _____
Date: _____

Vocabulary Juggle Puzzle

Directions: Change the order of the letters to find the original word. All words may be found in the **vocabulary lists.**

1. AFNU   _____

2. RFRAEOB   _____

3. ASUIRMTNAO   _____

4. TFTGIRONH   _____

5. ASRYT   _____

6. NHMOSA   _____

7. SCNREIT   _____

8. OCOITNNROA   _____

9. NINOTSNCTIAA   _____

10. LDLBAEOPER   _____

11. DWEBOARR   _____

12. WBRELO   _____

13. ANDAI   _____

14. NMSNOII   _____

15. AENETTCHMNH   _____

16. UADESCRC   _____

17. SRGNIOTO   _____

The Magician's Nephew

Juggle Answer Key

1. AFNU	FAUN
2. RFRAEOB	FORBEAR
3. ASUIRMTNAO	SANATORIUM
4. TFTGIRONH	FORTNIGHT
5. ASRYT	SATYR
6. NHMOSA	HANSOM
7. SCNREIT	CISTERN
8. OCOITNNROA	CORONATION
9. NINOTSNCTIAA	INCANTATIONS
10. LDLBAEOPER	DEPLORABLE
11. DWEBOARR	WARDROBE
12. WBRELO	BOWLER
13. ANDAI	NAIAD
14. NMSNOII	MINIONS
15. AENETTCHMNH	ENCHANTMENT
16. UADESCRC	ACCURSED
17. SRGNIOTO	ROOSTING

The Magician's Nephew

Name: _____

Date: _____

Test

Matching: For each character, find the description that matches it and write the letter in the blank to the left of the character's name.

1. _____ Digory	**A.**	Gave a command to Digory
2. _____ Polly	**B.**	Was a real Magician
3. _____ Uncle Andrew	**C.**	A winged animal
4. _____ Jadis	**D.**	Wanted to explore other worlds
5. _____ Cabby	**E.**	Was planted and watered
6. _____ Aslan	**F.**	Suggested they sing a hymn
7. _____ Fledge	**G.**	Was the first to arrive in the Wood

Fill in the Blanks: Read each sentence. Find the word from the word bank that makes the sentence correct.

Word Bank

Charn	roaring	thicket	green	Despairing Word	planted	rings
traveled	Narnia	mother	tree	Uncle Andrew	singing	Digory
Cabby	tempted	yellow	Aslan	hammer	toffee	empty
clay	Deplorable Word	Polly	heal	palace	ill	walk
aunt	grew	Jadis	dust	evil	garden	Wood
eat	sang	fool	bell	apple	created	talk

1. _____ lived with his aunt and uncle because his _____ was _____.

2. _____ found Digory and _____ in his study.

3. Uncle Andrew made _____ out of magic _____.

4. The _____ ring took Digory to a _____.

5. Digory hit a golden _____ with a _____ .

6. Jadis destroyed _____ with the _____ .

7. _____ grabbed Polly's hair and _____ with the children.

8. The group arrived in an _____ world.

9. Aslan _____ a new world by _____ .

10. _____ gave some animals the ability to _____ .

11. Uncle Andrew heard _____ when Aslan spoke.

12. Aslan made the _____ the King of _____ .

13. Digory went to a _____ to get an _____ .

14. Digory was _____ to _____ the apple.

15. Digory _____ the apple, and it _____ into a _____ .

16. Aslan gave an apple to Digory to _____ his mother.

<u>**Short Answer:**</u> Answer each question. Remember to restate the question in the answer.

1. What did Jadis want to do with Digory and Polly? Why? (Chap 5) _____

_____

_____

_____

2. When a lady brought grapes for Digory's mother, what did he begin thinking about? (Chap 7) _____

_____

_____

3. Aslan asked Digory how the Witch had come to Narnia. What was Digory's answer? (Chap 11)

_____

_____

_____

4. What was the purpose of the tree Digory planted, and how did it work? (Chap 14) _____

_____

_____

_____

A Bit More...

Explain what you thought of the book and why. Be specific.

_____

_____

_____

_____

_____

_____

_____

_____

Logos School Literature Series

The Magician's Nephew

Test Answer Key

Matching

1. D   2. G   3. E   4. B   5. F   6. A   7. C

Fill in the Blanks

1. Digory; mother; ill
2. Uncle Andrew; Polly
3. rings; dust
4. green; Wood
5. bell; hammer
6. Charn; Deplorable Word
7. Jadis; traveled
8. empty
9. created; singing
10. Aslan; talk
11. roaring
12. Cabby; Narnia
13. garden; apple
14. tempted; eat
15. planted; grew; tree
16. heal

Short Answer

1. Jadis wanted Digory and Polly to take her to their world so she could rule it.

2. When a lady brought grapes for Digory's mother, he began to think about going to another world and finding fruit that would cure his mother.

3. When Aslan asked Digory how the Witch had come to Narnia, Digory answered that he had brought her by using the magic rings after he had woken her up with the golden bell.

4. The purpose of the tree Digory planted was to protect Narnia from the Witch. She would not come near because the smell of the tree was despair to her.